Jesus: A ~~Vision~~

Marcus J. Borg

Leader's Guide

HarperSanFrancisco
A Division of HarperCollins*Publishers*

Leader's Guide prepared by Harriet Crosby

FIRST EDITION

Library of Congress Cataloging-in-Publication Data for original title
Borg, Marcus J.
   Jesus: a new vision: spirit, culture, and the life of discipleship /
   Marcus J. Borg
      p. cm.
   Reprint. Originally published: San Francisco: Harper & Row, © 1987.
   Includes bibliographical references and indexes.
   ISBN 0-06-060814-5 (alk. paper)
   1. Jesus Christ—Person and offices. 2. Jesus Christ—Significance.
   I. Title.
[BT202.B644 1991]
232—dc20   91–55090

ISBN 0–06–060864–1 (Leader's Guide)

93 94 95 96 97 ❖ VICKS 10 9 8 7 6 5 4 3 2 1

Contents

Introduction

In *Jesus: A New Vision*, Marcus Borg states that Jesus as a historical figure has a direct impact on contemporary Christian faith and practice. He paints an exciting, surprising portrait of the historical Jesus, a Jewish charismatic profoundly in touch with the Spirit, who offered his culture a radical alternative to the political and social crises that threatened to destroy them.

Because Jesus was so in touch with the world of Spirit, contemporary followers of Jesus can experience his spiritual world in fresh, new ways. This Leader's Guide helps readers of *Jesus: A New Vision* integrate the historical Jesus into their personal and corporate lives. Participants in the six-week group will explore Jesus as charismatic, or person of Spirit; Jesus as healer; Jesus as sage; Jesus as founder; and Jesus as prophet. Each session contains discussion questions and exercises to help participants experience these various facets of the historical Jesus as living Savior. There are many opportunities for group members to share with one another their emerging new visions of Jesus, forming relationships that will last far beyond their six weeks of study together.

As always, the Leader's Guide is a flexible tool. If you are an experienced leader, feel free to add to the exercises or to adjust the time spent on various activities to fit the needs of your group.

Jesus: A New Vision will challenge and transform participants' experience of Jesus into a fresh, exciting encounter with the living Lord.

Starting an Adult Study Group and Using This Leader's Guide

Harper's series of Leader's Guides provides resources for small adult study groups. Each Guide is based on a widely read book by a well-known and knowledgeable author. The Guides supply suggestions for forming small groups and for leading the discussions and include discussion questions and other material that can be photocopied for participants.

Although designed for use in Christian churches of all denominations, Harper's Leader's Guides may also be used in other settings: neighborhood study groups, camps, retreat centers, colleges and seminaries, or continuing education classes.

Format

Harper's Leader's Guides have been planned as the basis for six weeks of one-hour sessions. This amount of time allows for depth and personal sharing, yet is a limited commitment, one that even busy adults find easy to make.

The Leader's Guides can also be adapted for use in other time frames. By combining sessions, you can discuss a book in four meetings. Or, by being very selective with questions, you can plan a single two-hour session. Another option is to use a Guide as the foundation for a weekend retreat: alternate the six hour-long sessions with recreation, rest, meals, and other activities.

Forming a Group

Choose a book that you think will be of interest to people in your congregation or other setting. Inform them of the upcoming opportunity through your parish newsletter and service announcements or by visiting existing groups and encouraging interested people to invite others. It may be helpful to plan a brief orientation meeting for those who want to be involved.

As few as three or four adults joined by a common interest can create an effective discussion group. If more than twelve people respond, they should probably be divided into smaller groups.

Participants should have access to the books at least a week before the first session. Books may be ordered through your local bookstore or from Customer Service, HarperSanFrancisco, 1160 Battery Street, San Francisco, CA 94111, or call toll-free: 800-328-5125. Plan to allow about six weeks for delivery.

When you distribute books, participants should also receive photocopies of "Material for Group Distribution" found at the back of the Leader's Guide (permission has been granted for leaders to make photocopies of this section). You may want to hand out all the material before the first session, or you may distribute the information one session at a time.

Ask participants to take time to look over the information before coming to a meeting. The prepared discussion questions will serve as a medium for sharing insights, clarifying questions, and reinforcing learning.

Helps for Leaders

1. Be clear in announcing the time and place of the first meeting. If possible, meet in a pleasant, comfortable room where chairs can be set in a circle. This usually encourages more discussion than a formal classroom setting does.

2. Choose a leadership style: one person may direct the discussion in all six sessions, or there may be two people who work together every session or alternate sessions. Leadership may also be rotated among the participants.

3. "Materials for Group Distribution," found at the back of the Guide, can be photocopied for your group.

4. The Leader's Guide contains several kinds of questions. Some focus on what the book says. Do not neglect these, as they are

basic to intelligent discussion. There are also good questions for drawing more reluctant members into the conversation. Others deal with the meaning and implications of the author's words. And some ask participants to share their experiences, ideas, and feelings.

5. In the Leader's Guide you will find sample responses to the questions. Do not consider these to be the "right answers." They are only suggested responses, which often direct you to particular passages in the book. Be open to participants' responses that may stray from these suggested answers.

6. Don't feel you have to complete all the questions and suggested activities in the Leader's Guide. Choose only those that seem most important to your group.

7. Try to avoid having one or two people monopolize the discussion. Encourage quiet participants to share their thoughts.

8. If the group spends too much time on one question, or if it goes off on a tangent, gently move the discussion on to another question.

9. Encourage openness and trust in the group by being willing to share your own thoughts. Try to establish an atmosphere in which all ideas are treated with respect and seriousness.

10. The Leader's Guide contains some suggestions for group process. Experiment with these, and feel free to adapt them to your particular group.

Preparing for Session 1

If you have not already done so, read through *Jesus: A New Vision*, so you have an overview of the whole book. Also read the entire Leader's Guide.

At least a week before the first group session, arrange to give each participant a copy of *Jesus: A New Vision* and a photocopy of the discussion guide for session 1, located at the back of this Guide. You may wish to hand out all the "Materials for Group Distribution" at this time.

If possible, hold a brief meeting to hand out supplies and offer the following information. If this is not practical, arrange a time for each participant to pick up materials. Be sure the time and place of the first meeting is clear to everyone.

Ask participants to read pages 1 through 8 of *Jesus: A New Vision* and answer the discussion questions for session 1 *before* the group meets. You need not feel you must discuss all the questions for any session, but it is helpful if all participants have dealt with them privately before the small-group meeting.

Ask members to bring writing paper and pen or pencil to all sessions. Suggest they might find it helpful and convenient to keep a special notebook to record responses to discussion questions and keep notes in for each session.

Reread pages 1 through 8 of *Jesus: A New Vision* and work through the discussion questions for session 1. If you answer the questions before you consult the suggested responses in the Leader's Guide, you will be better prepared to lead the group.

Check the "Session Materials" list for session 1, and gather all needed supplies.

Session 1: The Historical Jesus

Jesus: A New Vision, Preface and pages 1 through 8

Session Objectives

- To introduce the concept of the historical Jesus
- To identify and articulate personal images of Jesus
- To begin to get to know other people in the group

Session Materials

- Copies of *Jesus: A New Vision*
- Poster paper, easel, and markers or chalkboard and chalk
- Pen and paper
- Photocopies of the discussion guide for session 2 for distribution to each member

Opening

Greet each person as he or she arrives. Be sure that everyone has a copy of *Jesus: A New Vision* and a photocopy of the discussion questions for session 1.

When the group has gathered, ask participants to pair off; suggest they choose a person they don't know very well. If there is an uneven number in the group, complete the remaining pair yourself.

Give the pairs ten minutes to interview each other in preparation for introducing each other to the group. In addition to learning a name and brief personal background, have participants ask the following questions:

- Why did you come to this group?
- What do you hope to learn about Jesus?

When the interviewing is completed, reassemble the group and let each person briefly (in one or two minutes) introduce his or her partner and explain why he or she came to a group studying Jesus.

Practicing Together

At the top of the chalkboard or poster paper on the easel, write "My Personal Images of Jesus."

Ask the group members to suggest words or phrases that describe their personal images of Jesus. For example, some words or phrases may include:

- ❑ Meek and mild
- ❑ Gentle
- ❑ Prophet
- ❑ Teacher
- ❑ Lover of my soul
- ❑ Savior

This is a brainstorming exercise, so have participants quickly offer words describing Jesus, without discussion or elaboration. Record the words on the easel paper or chalkboard as people speak.

After ten minutes, conclude the exercise. Tell the group you are going to save this paper and discuss it during session 6, the last session. If you used a chalkboard to complete this exercise, record the words and phrases on paper after the session, and save it.

Reflecting Together

Ask everyone to open *Jesus: A New Vision* to the Preface and silently skim through the Preface and pages 1 through 8 of the Introduction. This material should have been read by participants prior to the session, so this should take just three to five minutes.

Begin the discussion of the Preface and Introduction. Allow fifteen minutes for discussion.

1.   What is the difference between the Gospel of Mark and the Gospel of John regarding the image of Jesus?

In John's Gospel, Jesus proclaims his divine identity and saving purpose. In Mark's Gospel, Jesus kept his messiahship a secret during his ministry. "In short, in Mark the proclamation of Jesus' own identity and of the saving purpose of his death was not the message of Jesus. He did not proclaim himself" (p. 5).

2.   Contrast the "risen Christ" with the "historical Jesus."

An understanding and experience of the risen Christ as divine being was developed after Easter by the early Church, who looked back on the events surrounding Jesus. The historical Jesus is the human figure prior to the first Easter, who lived during a particular time in history.

Looking Ahead

During the last five minutes of the session, tell participants that they will be reading *Jesus: A New Vision* not only to understand, but to *experience* the historical Jesus. During the next five weeks they will experience him in prayer, song and music, art and icons, poetry and literature.

To begin their experience of the historical Jesus, ask participants to bring to session 2 an image of Jesus that is meaningful to them. These images may include icons, crosses, crucifixes, small statues, Sunday school art, contemporary poster art, fine art, folk art, or original art created by them. If group members do not have such art or objects at home, suggest they explore local religious bookstores, many of which carry posters, icons, and religious objects. Also suggest researching the art sections of local libraries and checking out books with meaningful images of Jesus.

Tell participants that these objects/art will form the basis for the next session's exercise.

Announce the time and place of your next meeting. Ask participants to finish the Introduction and also read chapters 2 and 3 of *Jesus: A New Vision*. Ask them to reflect on the questions in the photocopied discussion guide for session 2. Distribute these if you haven't already done so.

Closing

You may close the session with the following prayer, asking participants to read aloud:

> Lord Jesus,
> We gather together to follow you.
> May your Spirit touch each heart and mind,
>   opening each life to the experience of your
>   presence.
> To you, O Lord of history, be honor and glory,
>   now and forever.
> Amen.

Session 2: Jesus as Charismatic

Jesus: A New Vision, pages 8 through 21 and chapters 2 and 3

Session Objectives

- To explore and experience the world of Spirit
- To understand the historical Jesus as a Jewish charismatic

Session Materials

- Copies of *Jesus: A New Vision* for newcomers
- Poster paper, easel, and markers or chalkboard and chalk
- Extra copies of the discussion guide for session 2
- Photocopies of the discussion guide for session 3

Opening

If any newcomers have joined the group, introduce them to the others. Be sure each has a copy of *Jesus: A New Vision* and a photocopy of the discussion guide.

Tell participants that this week will be focused on Jesus as a powerful charismatic figure.

Reflecting Together

Begin discussion of the end of the Introduction through chapter 3 of *Jesus: A New Vision* using the questions below. Allow about fifteen minutes for discussion.

1. **Describe the "world of Spirit."**
   It is another reality that was a part of primordial cultures including Judaism. The world of Spirit is nonmaterial, charged with energy and power. This "other world" is not an object of belief, but an element of religious experience (pp. 25–27).

2. Why is it so difficult for us to experience the world of Spirit as reality?

Answers may vary. But part of the answer lies in our contemporary psychological definition of reality—we tend to view the spiritual realm as merely an extension (or aberration) of the human psyche without any reality of its own (pp. 32–34).

3. Outline and briefly discuss the facets of Jesus' experience of the Spirit world and his connection to the Jewish charismatic tradition.

Write the following aspects of Jesus' spiritual experience on the chalkboard or easel paper to aid discussion: visions, prayer, the Spirit of the Lord, the impression Jesus made on others, Jesus' authority, the Transfiguration, and Jesus' sense of identity (pp. 42–50). You may want to stress that *charismatic* here does not mean Pentecostal and is not limited to phenomena like speaking in tongues.

4. What additional insights have you gained from *Jesus: A New Vision*? What questions do you have?

Answers will vary. Write down the questions and save them for future sessions.

Practicing Together

Each participant should have brought an image of the historical Jesus that is meaningful to him or her—objects such as icons, crucifixes, crosses, statues, prints, posters, or pieces of original art.

During the next twenty minutes, ask participants to share their images of Jesus with the group. Ask them the following questions:

• Why is this particular image of Jesus meaningful to you?

• How does this image show Jesus' experience of or connection to the world of Spirit?

After all participants have shared their images of Jesus, ask them to take their images home and find a special place for them there, perhaps in the garden. Preferably it should be a private, quiet place. Suggest that they make this a place of prayer and meditation for the next five weeks. If some images were borrowed and must be returned before the five weeks end, suggest that participants find something to keep in their quiet place to help draw the image of Jesus to their mind.

Prepare participants to spend the next fifteen minutes practicing a form of contemplative prayer they may use at home. Remember to save ten minutes at the end of the session for "Looking Ahead" and "Closing."

First, read the following excerpts from *Jesus: A New Vision:*

> Among the reasons that we in the modern world have difficulty giving credence to the reality of Spirit is the disappearance of the deeper forms of prayer from our experience. . . . Beyond [the more common forms of verbal prayer] are deeper levels of prayer characterized by internal silence . . . one sits quietly in the presence of God. Typically called contemplation or meditation, its deepest levels are described as a communion or union with God. . . . At the heart of Jesus' prayer life was the experience of communion with God. (pp. 43, 44, and 45)

Then ask participants to place their images in front of them, so they can focus their eyes comfortably there. Have everyone sit in a relaxed position, with both feet on the floor and hands resting lightly in his or her lap.

Explain that they will spend the next several minutes sitting quietly in the presence of God while focusing their eyes on the image of Jesus. As their eyes rest on the image of Jesus, participants should take deep, relaxed, even breaths. Tell them there are two ways they may practice contemplative prayer.

- They may sit quietly offering up in prayer whatever comes to mind by breathing in the presence of God and breathing out a brief prayer—this process of inhaling God's presence and exhaling a prayer should be repeated until the time is up.

- Or they may use the following contemplative prayer (called the "Jesus Prayer") practiced by the Church over the centuries: "Lord Jesus Christ, have mercy on me, a sinner."

  Participants using this ancient prayer may break it up into smaller pieces. For example, they may simply pray, "Lord Jesus Christ" or "Have mercy on me" or "Lord Jesus Christ, have mercy." Whether they pray the whole "Jesus Prayer" or a portion of it, participants should breathe in the presence of God and breathe out the "Jesus Prayer."

When the time is up, very gently call participants' attention back to the group.

Looking Ahead

Announce the time and place of the next meeting. Ask participants to read chapter 4 in *Jesus: A New Vision.*

Ask them to skim through any of the four Gospels and select their favorite story of Jesus healing someone. Ask them to bring their selection to share with the group at the next meeting.

Ask participants to continue practicing contemplative prayer using their images of Jesus in a special place at home or in the garden. Tell them that volunteers will later be asked to share how contemplative prayer is shaping their experience of Jesus and the world of Spirit.

Distribute photocopies of the discussion guide for session 3 if you have not already done so.

Closing

You may use the following prayer to close this session, asking participants to read aloud:

> Lord Jesus Christ,
> You are our door to the world of Spirit.

Help us to let go of our old beliefs about reality
that keep us separated from you.
May your Spirit breathe through us this week,
giving us a new vision of you.
For we pray in your name. Amen.

Session 3: Jesus as Healer

Jesus: A New Vision, chapter 4

Session Objectives

• To understand the historical Jesus as a healer

• To begin experiencing Jesus as healer

Session Materials

• Bibles for everyone

• Extra photocopies of the discussion guide for session 3

• A watch with a second hand

• Photocopies of the discussion guide for session 4

Opening

Tell participants that this session will focus on the importance of the historical Jesus as a healer and that they will begin to experience Jesus as healer in their own lives.

Last week, participants were asked to skim through the Gospels and select their favorite story of Jesus healing someone. During the next ten minutes, distribute the Bibles and ask participants to read their favorite story of Jesus as healer and briefly explain why that particular story is meaningful to them.

Reflecting Together

Begin discussion of chapter 4 of *Jesus: A New Vision* using the questions below. Allow fifteen minutes for discussion.

1. Why are the stories of Jesus healing people important to our understanding of the historical Jesus?

They are important because Jesus' miracle healings were channels of his charismatic powers. They demonstrated

Jesus' connection with the world of Spirit. Miracles of healings (and other mighty deeds) firmly anchored Jesus in the history of the Jewish charismatic tradition (pp. 65–67).

2. Briefly discuss the difference between "miracles as part of the *history of Jesus*" and "miracles as part of the *story of Jesus*."

Answers should include the following: Jesus' work as healer and exorcist anchored him firmly in the tradition and *history* of Jewish charismatics, those who directly experienced the power of God from the world of Spirit. Miracles of healing and exorcisms are therefore historical. Jesus' other mighty deeds are the early Church's *story* about Jesus, and not primarily part of the history of Jesus himself. These other mighty deeds point *beyond* Jesus—back in time to key liberating moments in Israel's past and into the future experience of the Church (pp. 60–70).

3. Marcus Borg writes, "In their historical context, the miracles of Jesus do not 'prove' that he was divine" (p. 70). Some of us may have been taught in Sunday school that the miracles of Jesus, especially the healing miracles, prove Jesus was divine. How does this sentence challenge our traditional image of Jesus? How do you feel about Jesus' miracles not being proof of divinity?

Participants may have a variety of responses. Allow people to express feelings and opinions about Borg's statement, and let the discussion range freely for a while.

Responses may include something like: "If the healing miracles are not proof of Jesus' divinity, how can I be sure about Jesus as the Son of God at all?" Or, "I've always had difficulty believing in Jesus as a healer and miracle worker—this gives me a new, helpful image of Jesus." Or, "Understanding Jesus as a healer and miracle worker anchors him in history for me, and he becomes more 'real.'"

4. At this point in your study, what questions or comments do you have?

Responses will vary. Keep a list of questions for later if you run out of time to discuss them all.

Practicing Together

Allow twenty-five minutes for the following exercise. Begin by slowly reading aloud Mark 2:1–12. Explain to participants that, using guided imagery, they will practice experiencing Jesus as healer in their own lives. Tell them this guided imagery exercise is simply a technique to help them use their imaginations to enter the biblical text and experience Jesus for themselves in the present. Remember to save ten minutes at the end of the session for "Looking Ahead" and "Closing."

Ask participants to enter a contemporary story of the healing of the paralytic by participating in the following guided imagery exercise taken from *The Healing Presence* by Thomas A. Droege. Read the following section slowly in a gentle, measured voice, pausing slightly when you see a sequence of dots (. . .) or when otherwise indicated; use a watch with a second hand to keep track of the timed pauses.

A Guided Imagery: Healing the Paralytic in You

Be as relaxed as you can where you are sitting . . . releasing all the tension within your body . . . feeling the tension melt away like snow under the rays of a warm sun . . . letting your eyes close or keeping them focused on one particular spot to keep yourself from being distracted by what is going on outside you . . . breathing naturally and slowly . . . breathing in . . . breathing out . . . breathing in . . . breathing out . . . feeling the relaxation deepening . . . letting your awareness shift from what is happening outside you to what is happening within you.

(Pause for 30 seconds)

In your mind's eye imagine yourself either partially or completely paralyzed. You can decide how complete the paralysis is, but it should be severe enough to keep you bedfast and dependent on others for your care. Imagine what you would look like and how you would feel after a prolonged period of being confined to bed and dependent on others for your care. I will give you a moment to enter deeply and fully into that scene until you are that paralyzed person and view this scene from within that paralyzed body.

(Pause for 2 minutes)

From within this experience of yourself as paralyzed, ask yourself the question, "Who is the paralytic within me? What resonates most fully with the feeling of being paralyzed?" Are there parts of your body that are stiff, no longer functioning smoothly? Is there something in your behavior that is paralyzed, making it difficult for you to assert yourself or reach out to someone whose support you need? Or maybe you are aware of a rigidity in your behavior that makes you resistant to change. I'll give you a moment to get in touch with the paralytic in you.

(Pause for 1 minute)

Imagine that Jesus was born in this century rather than the first century. He has a reputation as a modern-day healer, and you have just heard that he is coming to the town where you live. How would you react to the news of his coming? How do you feel about healers and the claims made by them? Are you the kind of person who would go to a healer? If Jesus were your contemporary, how would he be the same, and how would he be different, from modern-day healers? Take a moment to reflect on the healing presence of Jesus and what he might do for the paralytic in you.

(Pause for 1 minute)

If you think Jesus can be of some help to you, imagine how you can get to him, enlisting whatever support you need to accomplish that. I'll give you a moment to let that unfold in your mind.

(Pause for 1 minute)

Imagine yourself in the presence of Jesus, surrounded by many people who are eager to see and hear him. It can be a place of your choosing, indoors or outdoors, anyplace that seems appropriate to you. Do you feel you have a right to be there? What are your expectations? Are you hopeful or skeptical, or maybe both at the same time? Look at the face of Jesus as he turns to you. What is the expression on his face as he looks at you, and how does that make you feel? What do you want to ask him?

(Pause for 30 seconds)

Before you can ask or say anything, Jesus says to you: "My child, your sins are forgiven." Is that what you were going to request from him? What do you suppose prompted him to say that? Is he suggesting that you are responsible for your paralysis? How might that be? Is it possible that at some level you really chose to be this way, that you have contributed to your condition of powerlessness? Or is he trying to tell you that your sins are your chief problem, not your paralysis? "My child, your sins are forgiven. My child, your sins are forgiven." Let these words echo through your mind as you repeat them to yourself, "My child, your sins are forgiven."

(Pause for 30 seconds)

Suddenly you are aware that a controversy has broken out between Jesus and the church leaders who are there. They are critical of him for forgiving sins when he's not even ordained, much less divine. How are you feeling as that battle wages? Give yourself a voice to respond to what is happening. Let that voice be an expression of your need and your faith.

(Pause for 30 seconds)

Jesus concludes the argument by telling his critics that he will demonstrate that he has power to forgive sins. Imagine that Jesus turns to you and speaks directly to the paralysis in you, telling you what you need to know and do about that paralysis. Then respond to what Jesus tells you in a manner that feels right to you. Let that scene unfold naturally and then bring it to a close in any way that seems appropriate to you.

(Pause for 1 to 2 minutes)

As you are ready, open your eyes and reorient yourself to this room and its surroundings, with a feeling of freedom and spontaneity in body, mind and spirit.

After all have opened their eyes, ask volunteers to briefly share whether they thought this exercise was a valuable tool in experiencing Jesus as healer.

Looking Ahead

Ask participants to practice guided imagery at home, using the story of the paralytic or the favorite healing text they selected and shared this evening. Also encourage participants to continue practicing contemplative prayer, focusing on their images of Jesus or using the "Jesus Prayer."

Ask participants to read chapters 5 and 6 of *Jesus: A New Vision* for next week. Also request that they bring to the next session a collection of newspapers and various magazines to use in the exercise.

If you have not already done so, distribute the discussion guide for session 4.

Closing

You may use the following prayer to close this session, asking participants to read aloud:

> Lord Jesus Christ,
> You are the great healer of our lives.

Grant us the experience of knowing the power
of your healing presence in our lives and in the
lives of those we love.
For we want to follow you in the world of
Spirit.
In your name, we pray. Amen.

Session 4: Jesus as Sage

Jesus: A New Vision, chapters 5 and 6

Session Objectives

- To understand Jesus as sage and cultural critic of his time
- To understand the social world in which Jesus lived and taught
- To begin to identify the conventional wisdom of our own culture in contrast to Jesus' teaching

Session Materials

- A variety of newspapers and magazines in case others forgot
- Photocopies of the discussion guide for session 5

Opening

During the first five minutes of the session, ask volunteers to share their experiences in contemplative prayer or guided imagery using the Bible. You may wish to ask them the following questions to encourage sharing:

- Has practicing contemplative prayer or guided imagery been relatively easy to incorporate into your life, or do you find these practices difficult? Explain.

- How has practicing contemplative prayer or guided imagery changed your experience of Jesus and/or the world of Spirit?

Last week, participants were asked to bring newspapers and magazines to this session. Collect the magazines and newspapers and put them on the floor in the middle of the circle.

Tell participants that this week's focus is on Jesus' social world and his role as sage.

Reflecting Together

Begin discussion of *Jesus: A New Vision*, chapters 5 and 6, using the questions below. Allow twenty minutes for discussion.

1. According to Borg, what is "conventional wisdom" in a culture?

Conventional wisdom consists of widely shared assumptions about life, convictions, and ways of behavior so taken for granted as to be basically unquestioned (p. 81).

2. Discuss the characteristics of first-century Jewish conventional wisdom and how it was challenged by crisis.

Jewish conventional wisdom in the first century was grounded in Torah and taught by sages. It held that reality was organized on rewards and punishments, and it placed great emphasis on identity, particularly by distinguishing the behavior of the righteous and the wicked.

The crisis to Jewish conventional wisdom and Torah came about through taxation under Roman law. Many people could not afford to pay both the tithes commanded by Torah and the Roman tax. Because the Roman tax was enforced by the law but Jewish tithes were not, a large class of nonobservant Jews was created. This challenged conventional wisdom's roots in Torah, the reality of rewards and punishments, and forced many Jews to abandon the path of the "righteous" (pp. 81–86).

3. What is "the politics of holiness"?

It is a response to the crisis of Roman occupation that emphasized "holiness" as the paradigm by which Torah was interpreted. The politics of holiness was characterized by separation: clean and unclean, pure and defiled, Jew and Gentile, righteous and sinner (pp. 86–87).

4. Contrast "the broad way" with "the narrow way" in Jesus' teaching as a sage.

The broad way is conventional wisdom that focuses on the security and identity offered by culture instead of centering on God. The broad way of conventional wisdom in Jesus' time focused on family as a source of identity and financial security; wealth and possessions as signs of blessing and righteousness; honor as the community's recognition of achievement, by the standards of conventional wisdom; and religion as a means of seeking both security and an honorable identity, instead of a way of centering on God.

The narrow way is Jesus' challenge to conventional wisdom—it is the path of transformation. The narrow way requires "a new heart," a change at the deepest level of self, centered on God (in contrast to centering on cultural security and identity). This radical recentering on God involves "the path of death," a dying of the self as the center of its own concern and a dying to the world as the center of security and identity. This radical centering on God "is an *invitation* to see things as they really are—namely, at the heart of everything is a reality that is in love with us" (p. 115; see pp. 104–15.)

Practicing Together

Allow thirty minutes for the following exercise. Divide the group into pairs. Have one person from each couple choose a few magazines and newspapers from the center of the circle. When each pair has selected its periodicals, ask participants to skim through articles, headlines, editorials, and advertisements. Their goal is to identify three characteristics of conventional wisdom at work in our own culture, as evident in these magazines and newspapers.

For example, in glancing through a magazine, a pair of participants finds an advertisement for a luxury car. They may de-
`de the ad characterizes our culture's conventional wisdom in
` of the following ways: that upward mobility is the goal of
rican life; or that identity with a certain class is motivation

for living; or that owning a luxury car is a way to feel young, and conventional wisdom prefers youth over maturity.

Each pair should then discuss and answer the following question:

*   How would Jesus as sage critique these characteristics of conventional wisdom, inviting us to travel the narrow way, the path of transformation?

After the pairs have identified characteristics of conventional wisdom and answered the question, bring participants back into a large group and ask one person from each pair to report briefly on its discussion. Remember to save five minutes for "Looking Ahead" and "Closing."

Looking Ahead

Ask participants to read chapters 7 and 8 of *Jesus: A New Vision*. Distribute photocopies of the discussion guide for session 5 if you have not already done so. Encourage participants to continue practicing contemplative prayer and guided imagery.

Closing

You may close this session with the following prayer, asking participants to read aloud:

> Lord Jesus Christ,
> Guide us through the narrow way.
> Help us to follow your path of transformation
>   in a culture tempting us to security.
> Grant us the grace to center on you and to experience your love.
> For we pray in your name. Amen.

Session 5: Jesus as Founder and Prophet

Jesus: A New Vision, chapters 7 and 8

Session Objectives

- To understand the movement Jesus founded
- To identify ourselves as heirs of that movement
- To understand Jesus' role as a prophet

Session Materials

- Hymnals for all participants
- Photocopies of the discussion guide for session 6

Opening

Tell participants that this session focuses on Jesus as a founder of a movement and as a prophet to his people. Discuss the following:

- What is a prophet?
- Are there men or women today who are prophets?
- Whom do you consider to be a contemporary prophet?

    Accept all answers.

Reflecting Together

Begin discussion of *Jesus: A New Vision*, chapters 7 and 8, by discussing the following questions. Allow twenty minutes for discussion.

1.   Marcus Borg writes, "We commonly think of Jesus as the founder of Christianity. But, strictly speaking, this is not historically true. Instead, his concern was the renewal of

Israel. . . . [H]e created a sectarian revitalization or renewal movement within Israel . . . whose purpose was the transformation of the Jewish social world" (p. 125). Describe the Jewish renewal movement that Jesus founded.

Answers should include: It was a charismatic movement, grounded in the Spirit; it was an itinerant movement, a group on the move; it was a movement characterized by joy in the presence of Jesus (pp. 126–29).

2. **What is the significance of compassion in the movement Jesus founded, and how was compassion expressed?**

Whereas first-century Judaism spoke primarily of the holiness of God, Jesus spoke primarily of the compassion of God. Jesus substituted a politics of compassion for a politics of holiness. Compassion was expressed by feasting with outcasts, threatening the division between purity and impurity, holy and not-holy, righteous and wicked; by associating with women; by preaching to the poor, challenging conventional wisdom's connection between righteousness and prosperity; by loving one's enemies and teaching nonviolence—Jesus' renewal movement functioned as a peace party in Israel; by spiritualizing elements of Jewish teaching, claiming that what truly matters is not the external practice or reality, but the internal or spiritual reality to which the external points (pp. 129–41).

3. **What is a prophet according to Borg?**

As messengers of God, the prophets charged Israel with violations of the covenant (the indictment), warned that the future would be filled with destruction (the threat), and called their people to change before it was too late (p. 152).

4. **What most surprised you about Jesus as prophet?**

Answers may include a variety of responses: that Jesus was concerned about Israel in his time, not the far distant future; that Jesus wasn't singling out the Pharisees with his prophetic indictment but was criticizing his culture's obsession with holiness; that Jesus really believed Israel could change and avoid disaster. In other words, Jesus wasn't making hard-and-fast predictions about the destruction of the temple but thought it could be avoided if Israel repented (pp. 157–65).

Practicing Together

Read the following quote from *Jesus: A New Vision:*

> The movement was marked by joy. . . . To be in the presence of Jesus was a joyous experience. . . . To be in the presence of Jesus was experienced as being in the presence of the Spirit which flowed through him. (pp. 128 and 129)

Explain to participants that we are heirs to the movement Jesus founded. We, too, experience joy in the presence of Jesus, the touch of the Spirit. One of the ways Christians regularly experience joy in the presence of Jesus is by singing hymns. The remainder of the time will be spent singing hymns together. (Distribute the hymnals to participants. Allow fifteen to thirty minutes to search for and sing hymns.)

Ask participants to search through their hymnals and select hymns to sing that reflect some of the themes discussed during this session: the compassion of Jesus; Jesus as founder; the power of the Spirit; Jesus' love for sinners and outcasts; Jesus as prophet, calling us to change or repent; the joy of Jesus' presence; and so on. For example, someone may choose "The Church's One Foundation" to sing about Jesus as founder; or "Amazing Grace" to sing about Jesus' love for outcasts; or "I've Got Joy, Joy, Joy, Joy . . . " about the believer's relationship to Christ.

You may wish to select a couple of hymns beforehand in case participants are slow getting started.

As each participant finds an appropriate hymn, sing it together. It is not necessary to have accompaniment—simply choose a comfortable beginning note and have everyone join in. If your group is not comfortable singing, read the words of the hymns in unison.

Looking Ahead

Ask participants to read the remainder of *Jesus: A New Vision,* chapters 9 and 10.

Explain to the group that the final session will be focused on a simple soup-and-salad meal taken together. Therefore, the group will need to meet in a place that has access to a kitchen. Ask participants to volunteer to bring soup, bread, salad, and wine or another beverage. Also discuss arrangements for providing eating utensils (plates, forks, knives, and soup spoons, glasses, and so on). Agree where and when you will meet; you may wish to meet at a mealtime for this final session. Emphasize that session 6 is only for participants who have met together over the past five weeks (or whatever time frame you have used to complete the Leader's Guide).

Ask participants to bring an item that represents how their image of Jesus has changed over the past five weeks. These may include poetry, a hymn or piece of music, a work of original art, the image of Jesus they began with, or a reading from a book.

In place of, or in addition to, the dinner, you could plan for your group to celebrate the Lord's Supper together in a way that is appropriate to your religious tradition.

If you have not already done so, distribute photocopies of the discussion guide for session 6.

Closing

You may use the following prayer to close this session, asking participants to read aloud:

> Lord Jesus Christ,
> All praise to you for founding a movement that
>   changed Israel and the world.
> But we especially give you thanks that you also
>   found each one of us and honored us with
>   your Spirit.

Help us to be faithful stewards of your movement, filled with compassion and the joy of
your Spirit.
For we pray in your name. Amen.

Session 6: Jesus as Experience

Jesus: A New Vision, chapters 9 and 10

Session Objectives

* To articulate how our vision of Jesus has changed over the past five weeks

* To experience the joy of being in Jesus' presence through table fellowship

Session Materials

* A potluck soup supper (brought by several participants)

* The brainstorming list from session 1, "My Personal Images of Jesus"

* An easel to display the brainstorming list or tape to attach it to a wall

Opening

Before everyone arrives, set up the brainstorming list, "My Personal Images of Jesus" (created in session 1), in a place where everyone can see it during dinner.

Call participants together at the table and read the following quote from *Jesus: A New Vision:*

> Eating together or "table fellowship"—not yet a ritual meal, but the festive act of sharing food and drink at a table—was one of the central characteristics of [Jesus'] movement. (p. 131)

Tell participants that this evening's dinner celebrates the presence of Jesus, the presence of the reality of the Spirit.

Ask everyone to join you in saying this prayer:

Lord Jesus Christ,
You are our doorway to the world of Spirit.
Help us to experience the love and wonder of
   your Spirit in the joy of your presence.
As we share this table fellowship this evening,
   usher us into the reality of your presence, the
   world of Spirit.
For we pray in your name. Amen.

Practicing Together

As participants eat, draw their attention to the brainstorming list, "My Personal Images of Jesus." Go around the table and ask each person to tell how his or her image of Jesus has changed over the course of the study. At this point, each may share how his or her vision or image of Jesus has changed by offering a poem, reading, piece of art, the image he or she began with, a hymn, or music.

After everyone has shared, read the following quote from *Jesus: A New Vision:*

> What if it is true that the world of our ordinary experience is but one level of reality, and that we are at all times surrounded by other dimensions of reality which we do not commonly experience? The claim that there really is a realm of Spirit is both exciting and oddly disconcerting. What if reality is other than we ever dreamed it could be? (p. 200)

Ask participants to discuss the questions Borg raises in this quote. There are no "right" answers—let the discussion range freely. To help the discussion along, you may want to ask:

• What does this vision of the historical Jesus mean for our personal and communal Christian experience?

Again, there are no "right" answers—let the discussion develop.

You may want to go back to some of the questions that were raised in earlier sessions and delve deeper into them in light of what everyone has learned during the study of *Jesus: A New Vision.*

Closing

After the meal is over, you may send the group home with the following benediction:

> May your journey with Jesus in the world of
>   Spirit be filled with wonder, love, and joy.
> Amen.

Materials for Group Distribution

Session 1: The Historical Jesus

Read *Jesus: A New Vision*, Preface and pages 1 through 8 of the Introduction.

1. What is the difference between the Gospel of Mark and the Gospel of John regarding the image of Jesus?

2. Contrast the "risen Christ" with the "historical Jesus."

Closing Prayer

> Lord Jesus,
> We gather together to follow you.
> May your Spirit touch each heart and mind,
>   opening each life to the experience of your
>   presence.
> To you, O Lord of history, be honor and glory
>   now and forever.
> Amen.

Session 2: Jesus as Charismatic

Read *Jesus: A New Vision*, pages 8 through 21 of the Introduction, chapter 2, "The Context," and chapter 3, "The Spirit-filled Experience of Jesus."

1. Describe the "world of Spirit."

2. Why is it so difficult for us to experience the world of Spirit as reality?

3. Outline and briefly discuss the facets of Jesus' experience of the Spirit world and his connection to the Jewish charismatic tradition.

4. What additional insights have you gained from *Jesus: A New Vision?* What questions do you have?

Exercise

At the end of session 1 you were asked to bring and share an image of Jesus that is meaningful to you. Prepare to discuss your image of Jesus with the group by answering the following questions:

- Why is this particular image of Jesus meaningful to you?

- How does this image show Jesus' experience of or connection to the world of Spirit?

Closing Prayer

Lord Jesus Christ,
You are our door to the world of Spirit.
Help us to let go of our old beliefs about reality
   that keep us separated from you.
May your Spirit breathe through us this week,
   giving us a new vision of you.
For we pray in your name. Amen.

Session 3: Jesus as Healer

Read *Jesus: A New Vision*, chapter 4, "The Power of the Spirit."

1. Why are the stories of Jesus healing people important to our understanding of the historical Jesus?

2. Briefly discuss the difference between "miracles as part of the *history of Jesus*" and "miracles as part of the *story of Jesus.*"

3. Marcus Borg writes, "In their historical context, the miracles of Jesus do not 'prove' that he was divine" (p. 70). Some of us may have been taught in Sunday school that the miracles of Jesus, especially the healing miracles, prove Jesus was divine. How does this sentence challenge our traditional image of Jesus? How do you feel about Jesus' miracles not being proof of divinity?

4. At this point in your study, what questions or comments do you have?

Exercise

During session 2 you were asked to skim the Gospels and select your favorite story of Jesus healing someone. Be prepared to share with the group why the story you chose is meaningful to you.

Closing Prayer

> Lord Jesus Christ,
> You are the great healer of our lives.
> Grant us the experience of knowing the power
>   of your healing presence in our lives and in the
>   lives of those we love.
> For we want to follow you in the world of
>   Spirit.
> In your name, we pray. Amen.

Session 4: Jesus as Sage

Read *Jesus: A New Vision*, chapter 5, "The Social World of Jesus," and chapter 6, "Jesus as Sage."

1. According to Borg, what is "conventional wisdom" in a culture?

2. Discuss the characteristics of first-century Jewish conventional wisdom and how it was challenged by crisis.

3. What is "the politics of holiness"?

4. Contrast "the broad way" with "the narrow way" in Jesus' teaching as a sage.

Exercise

During the last couple of weeks you have been encouraged to continue practicing contemplative prayer and/or guided imagery using the Bible. You may volunteer to share your experience with the group by answering the following questions:

- Has practicing contemplative prayer or guided imagery been relatively easy to incorporate into your life, or do you find these practices difficult? Explain.

- How has practicing contemplative prayer or guided imagery changed your experience of Jesus and/or the world of Spirit?

Closing Prayer

> Lord Jesus Christ,
> Guide us through the narrow way.
> Help us to follow your path of transformation
>   in a culture tempting us to security.
> Grant us the grace to center on you and to expe-
>   rience your love.
> For we pray in your name. Amen.

Session 5: Jesus as Founder and Prophet

Read *Jesus: A New Vision,* chapter 7, "Jesus as Revitalization Movement Founder," and chapter 8, "Jesus as Prophet."

1. Marcus Borg writes, "We commonly think of Jesus as the founder of Christianity. But, strictly speaking, this is not historically true. Instead, his concern was the renewal of Israel. . . . [H]e created a sectarian revitalization or renewal movement within Israel . . . whose purpose was the transformation of the Jewish social world" (p. 125). Describe the Jewish renewal movement that Jesus founded.

2. What is the significance of compassion in the movement Jesus founded, and how was compassion expressed?

3. What is a prophet according to Borg?

4. What most surprised you about Jesus as prophet?

Closing Prayer

> Lord Jesus Christ,
> All praise to you for founding a movement that
>   changed Israel and the world.
> But we especially give you thanks that you also
>   found each one of us and honored us with
>   your Spirit.
> Help us to be faithful stewards of your move-
>   ment, filled with compassion and the joy of
>   your Spirit.
> For we pray in your name. Amen.

Session 6: Jesus as Experience

Read *Jesus: A New Vision*, chapter 9, "Jesus as Challenge," and chapter 10, "Conclusion."

Session 6 is a potluck soup supper. Bring soup, salad, bread, or a beverage to share.

Also be prepared to share with the group how your image of Jesus has changed over the course of the study. You may demonstrate how it has changed by offering a poem, a reading, a piece of art, the image you began with in session 2, a hymn, or music.

Reflect on the following questions in preparation for general discussion during dinner:

> What if it is true that the world of our ordinary experience is but one level of reality, and that we are at all times surrounded by other dimensions of reality which we do not commonly experience? The claim that there really is a realm of Spirit is both exciting and oddly disconcerting. What if reality is other than we ever dreamed it could be? (p. 200)

What does this vision of the historical Jesus mean for our personal and communal Christian experience?

Opening Prayer

> Lord Jesus Christ,
> You are our doorway to the world of Spirit.
> Help us to experience the love and wonder of
>   your Spirit in the joy of your presence.
> As we share this table fellowship this evening,
>   usher us into the reality of your presence, the
>   world of Spirit.
> For we pray in your name. Amen.

Additional Resources for Leaders

Crossan, John Dominic. *The Historical Jesus: The Life of a Mediterranean Peasant.* San Francisco: HarperCollins, 1992. A professor of biblical studies at DePaul University uses the latest research methods to determine what can be known about the historical Jesus.

Droege, Thomas A. *The Healing Presence: Spiritual Exercises for Healing, Wellness, and Recovery.* San Francisco: HarperCollins, 1992. Droege provides guided imagery meditations for Christians, many of which are based on the Gospel accounts of Jesus as healer.

Kung, Hans. *On Being a Christian.* Garden City, NY: Doubleday, 1984. About half of this engaging and provocative "introduction" to the Christian faith is a substantial and lively treatment of the historical Jesus.

Muggeridge, Malcolm. *Jesus: The Man Who Lives.* San Francisco: Harper & Row, 1976. An illustrated history of the life of Jesus by a twentieth-century journalist and convert to Christianity.

Nouwen, Henri J. M. *Letters to Marc About Jesus.* San Francisco: Harper San Francisco, 1988. Letters of spiritual counsel, centered around Jesus and his teachings; see Harper's Leader's Guide series.

Pelikan, Jaroslav. *Jesus Through the Centuries.* New York: Harper & Row, 1987. Pelikan traces the various images and interpretations of Jesus through history.

Sampson, William P. *Meeting Jesus.* San Francisco: HarperCollins, 1991. A retreat leader helps readers use their imagination to experience Jesus in the Gospels.

Sanford, John A. *The Kingdom Within: The Inner Meaning of Jesus' Sayings,* rev. ed. San Francisco: Harper & Row, 1987. An Episcopal priest and Jungian psychologist offers fresh approaches to the truths of the Gospels; see Harper's Leader's Guide series.

Other Titles in Harper's Leader's Guide Series

You can order any of Harper's Leader's Guide Series books through your local bookstore or by writing to Torch Publishing Group, Harper San Francisco, 1160 Battery Street, San Francisco, CA 94111–1213, or call us toll-free: 800–328–5125.